MATH FOR

MINECRAFTERS

ADVENTURES IN
MULTIPLICATION & DIVISION
VOLUME 2

**Level Up Your Skills with New
Practice Problems and Activities!**

Sky Pony Press
New York

Copyright © 2021 by Hollan Publishing, Inc.
Minecraft® is a registered trademark of Notch Development AB.

The Minecraft game is copyright © Mojang AB.

Sky Pony Press books may be purchased in bulk at special discounts for sales promotion, corporate gifts, fund-raising, or educational purposes. Special editions can also be created to specifications. For details, contact the Special Sales Department, Sky Pony Press, 307 West 36th Street, 11th Floor, New York, NY 10018 or info@skyhorsepublishing.com.

Sky Pony® is a registered trademark of Skyhorse Publishing, Inc.®, a Delaware corporation.

Minecraft® is a registered trademark of Notch Development AB. The Minecraft game is copyright © Mojang AB.

Visit our website at www.skyponypress.com.

10 9 8 7 6 5 4 3 2 1

Library of Congress Cataloging-in-Publication Data is available on file.

Print ISBN: 978-1-5107-6622-8

Cover design by Brian Peterson
Interior design by Noora Cox
Cover and interior illustrations by Amanda Brack

Printed in China

A NOTE TO PARENTS

When you want to reinforce classroom skills at home, it's crucial to have kid-friendly learning materials. This *Math for Minecrafters: Adventures in Multiplication & Division, Volume 2* workbook transforms math practice into an irresistible adventure complete with diamond armor, zombie pigmen, ghasts, and skeletons. That means less arguing over homework and more fun overall.

Math for Minecrafters: Adventures in Multiplication & Division, Volume 2 is also fully aligned with National Common Core Standards for 3rd and 4th grade math. What does that mean, exactly? All of the problems in this book correspond to what your child is expected to learn in school. This eliminates confusion and builds confidence for greater homework-time success!

The primary focus of this Volume 2 workbook is math facts repetition and fluency. With enough supplemental practice, your child will commit the answers to common multiplication and division problems to memory and level up their math ability.

As the workbook progresses, the math problems become more advanced. Encourage your child to progress at his or her own pace. Learning is best when students are challenged, but not frustrated. What's most important is that your Minecrafter is engaged in his or her own learning.

Whether it's the joy of seeing their favorite game characters on every page or the thrill of solving challenging problems just like Steve and Alex, there is something in this workbook to entice even the most reluctant math student.

Happy adventuring!

MULTIPLICATION BY GROUPING

Write the multiplication sentence that matches the picture. Then solve the equation.

Example:

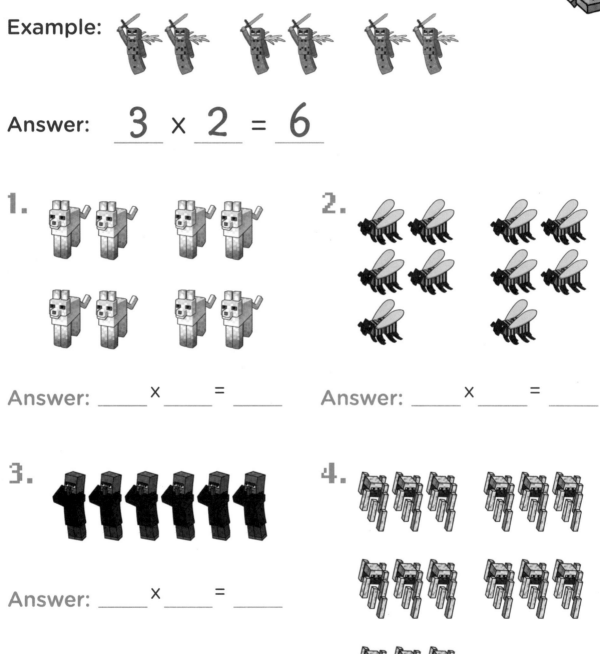

Answer: ___3___ × ___2___ = ___6___

1.

Answer: _____ × _____ = _____

2.

Answer: _____ × _____ = _____

3.

Answer: _____ × _____ = _____

4.

Answer: _____ × _____ = _____

MYSTERY MESSAGE WITH MULTIPLICATION

Multiply. Then use the letters to fill in the blanks below and reveal the answer to Steve's joke.

1. $3 \times 9 =$ _____ C

2. $4 \times 6 =$ _____ U

3. $10 \times 5 =$ _____ I

4. $6 \times 7 =$ _____ F

5. $7 \times 5 =$ _____ E

6. $2 \times 11 =$ _____ B

7. $5 \times 6 =$ _____ J

8. $9 \times 8 =$ _____ Y

Q: Where does Alex go to get her cart serviced?

Copy the letters from the answers above to solve the joke.

_____ _____ _____ _____ _____   _____ _____ _____ _____
 30   50   42   42   72   27   24   22   35

DROWNED'S GUIDE TO PLACE VALUE

Write the number on each drowned in expanded form in the space provided.

Example:  672

Answer:

600 + 70 + 2

1. 801

_____

2. 167

_____

3. 450

_____

4. 834

_____

5. 326

_____

6. 735

_____

MATH FACTS CHALLENGE

Find the pattern and fill in the empty spaces to help the villager escape the skeleton.

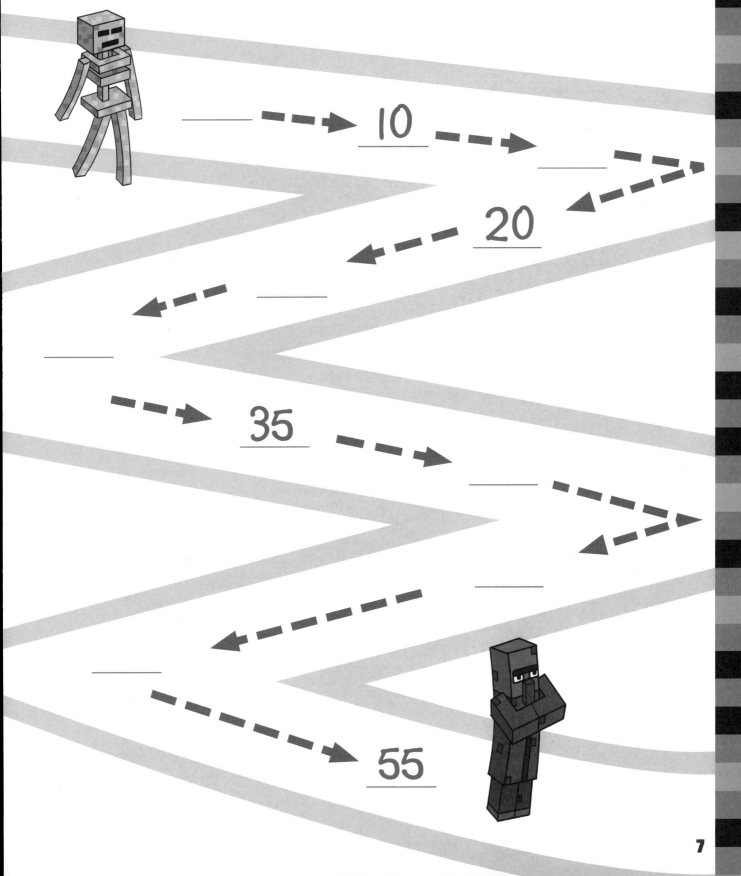

_____ → 10 → _____

20 ← _____

_____ ← _____

35 → _____ → _____

_____ ←

55 ← _____

MULTIPLICATION AND DIVISION
MYSTERY NUMBER

There is a number hidden behind these experience orbs. Divide the answer by the top number in the equation to find the mystery number.

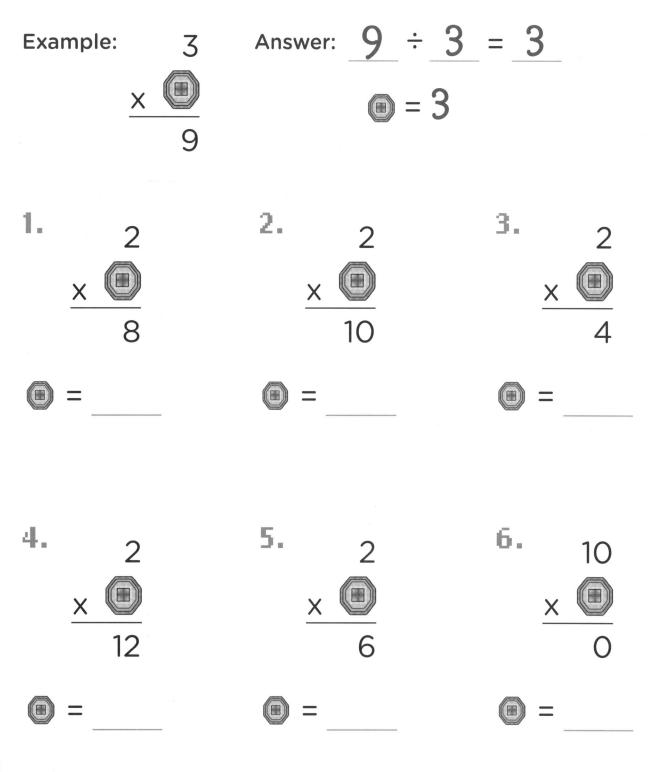

Example:

$$3 \times \text{orb} = 9$$

Answer: $9 \div 3 = 3$

$$\text{orb} = 3$$

1.
$$2 \times \text{orb} = 8$$

$$\text{orb} = \underline{\qquad}$$

2.
$$2 \times \text{orb} = 10$$

$$\text{orb} = \underline{\qquad}$$

3.
$$2 \times \text{orb} = 4$$

$$\text{orb} = \underline{\qquad}$$

4.
$$2 \times \text{orb} = 12$$

$$\text{orb} = \underline{\qquad}$$

5.
$$2 \times \text{orb} = 6$$

$$\text{orb} = \underline{\qquad}$$

6.
$$10 \times \text{orb} = 0$$

$$\text{orb} = \underline{\qquad}$$

MULTIPLICATION AND DIVISION
MYSTERY NUMBER

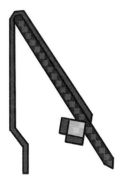

There is a number hidden behind these fish. Multiply the answer by the bottom number in the equation to find the mystery number.

Example:

Answer: $\underline{\ 2\ } \times \underline{\ 5\ } = \underline{\ 10\ }$

$$\begin{array}{r} \div\ 5 \\ \hline 2 \end{array}$$

🐟 = 10

1.

$$\begin{array}{r} \div\ 1 \\ \hline 7 \end{array}$$

🐟 = _____

2.

$$\begin{array}{r} \div\ 4 \\ \hline 2 \end{array}$$

🐟 = _____

3.

$$\begin{array}{r} \div\ 3 \\ \hline 2 \end{array}$$

🐟 = _____

4.

$$\begin{array}{r} \div\ 5 \\ \hline 1 \end{array}$$

🐟 = _____

5.

$$\begin{array}{r} \div\ 2 \\ \hline 4 \end{array}$$

🐟 = _____

6.

$$\begin{array}{r} \div\ 9 \\ \hline 1 \end{array}$$

🐟 = _____

MULTIPLICATION IN BASE 10

Multiply the numbers. Then fill in the place value chart. The first one is done for you.

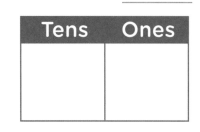

1. 8 × 7 = __56__

Tens	Ones
5	6

2. 5 × 7 = _____

Tens	Ones

3. 4 × 6 = _____

Tens	Ones

4. 9 × 7 = _____

Tens	Ones

5. 8 × 8 = _____

Tens	Ones

6. 3 × 6 = _____

Tens	Ones

7. 5 × 10 = _____

Tens	Ones

8. 3 × 9 = _____

Tens	Ones

DIVISION IN BASE 10

Divide the numbers. Then round the number up or down to the nearest ten. The first one is done for you.

Hint: Numbers 0, 1, 2, 3, and 4 round *down* to 0. Numbers 5, 6, 7, 8, and 9 round *up* to 10.

Divide	Solve it!	Round it!
1. $36 \div 6 =$	6	10
2. $72 \div 9 =$		
3. $24 \div 8 =$		
4. $12 \div 6 =$		
5. $56 \div 8 =$		
6. $42 \div 7 =$		
7. $10 \div 5 =$		
8. $28 \div 7 =$		

MULTIPLICATION BY GROUPING

Write the multiplication sentence that matches the picture. Then solve the equation. The first one is done for you.

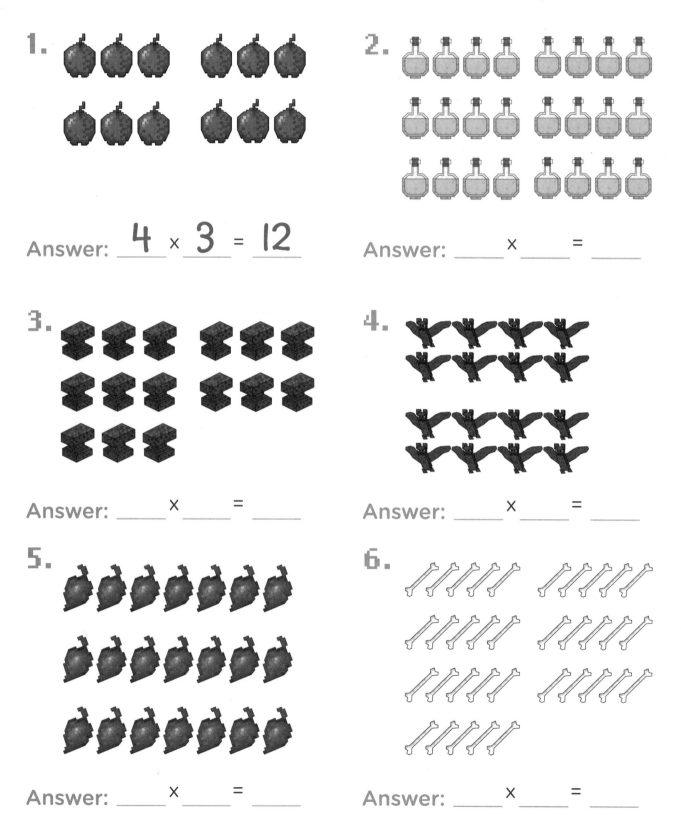

1.

Answer: $\underline{4} \times \underline{3} = \underline{12}$

2.

Answer: $\underline{} \times \underline{} = \underline{}$

3.

Answer: $\underline{} \times \underline{} = \underline{}$

4.

Answer: $\underline{} \times \underline{} = \underline{}$

5.

Answer: $\underline{} \times \underline{} = \underline{}$

6.

Answer: $\underline{} \times \underline{} = \underline{}$

MYSTERY MESSAGE WITH DIVISION

Divide. Then use the letters to fill in the blanks below and reveal the answer to Alex's riddle.

1. 18 ÷ 9 = _____ D

2. 42 ÷ 7 = _____ U

3. 50 ÷ 5 = _____ G

4. 35 ÷ 7 = _____ S

5. 81 ÷ 9 = _____ A

6. 30 ÷ 10 = _____ N

7. 56 ÷ 8 = _____ I

8. 28 ÷ 7 = _____ R

Q:What mobs make the best babysitters?

Copy the letters from the answers above to solve the joke.

_____ _____ _____ _____ _____ _____ _____ _____ _____
10   6   9   4   2   7   9   3   5

EVOKER'S GUIDE TO PLACE VALUE

Write the correct digit in the place value chart.
The first one is done for you.

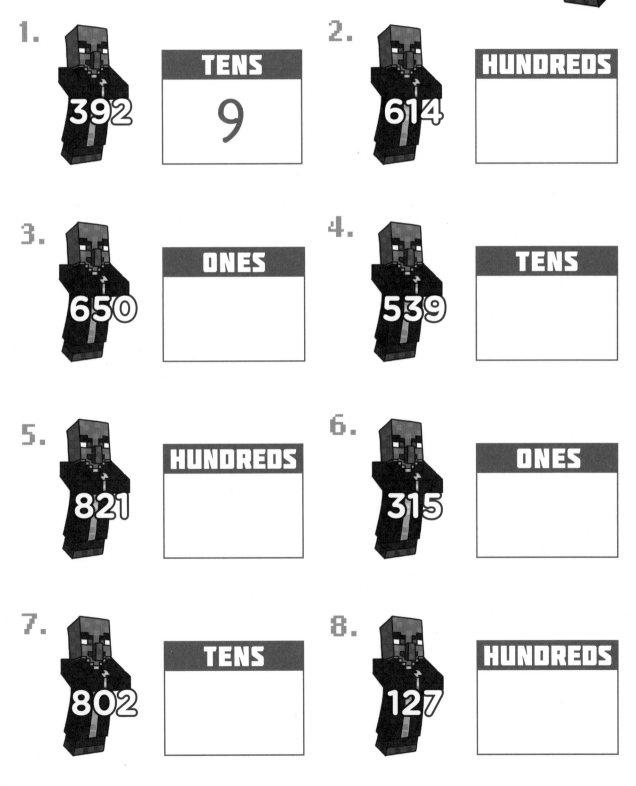

1. 392

TENS
9

2. 614

HUNDREDS

3. 650

ONES

4. 539

TENS

5. 821

HUNDREDS

6. 315

ONES

7. 802

TENS

8. 127

HUNDREDS

MATH FACTS CHALLENGE

Find the pattern and fill in the empty spaces to help Steve enchant his weapons and armor.

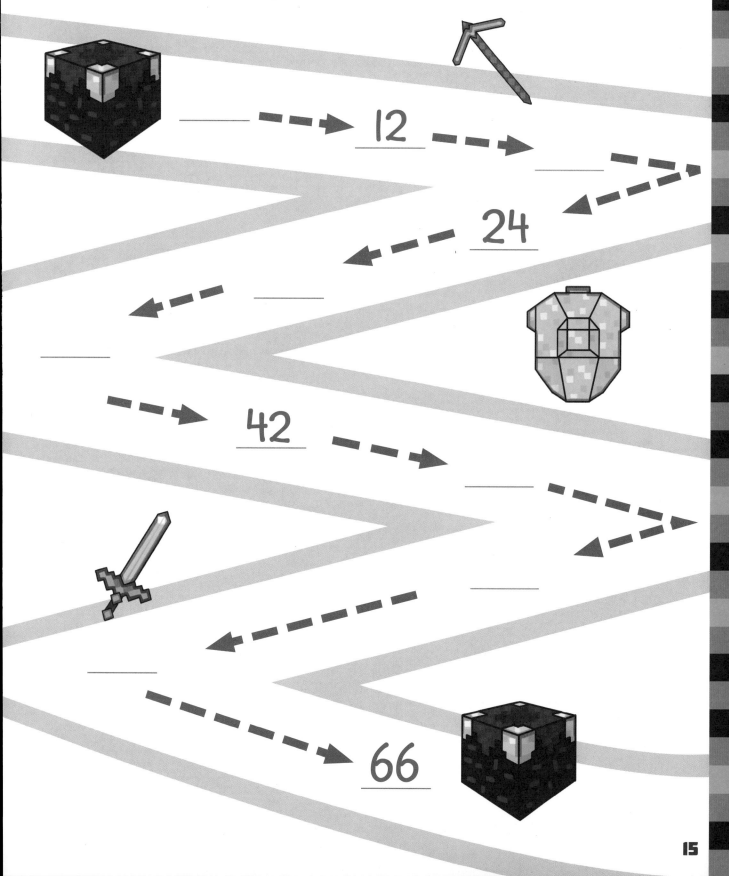

MULTIPLICATION AND DIVISION
MYSTERY NUMBER

There is a number hidden behind these diamonds. Divide the answer by the top number in the equation to find the mystery number. The first one is done for you.

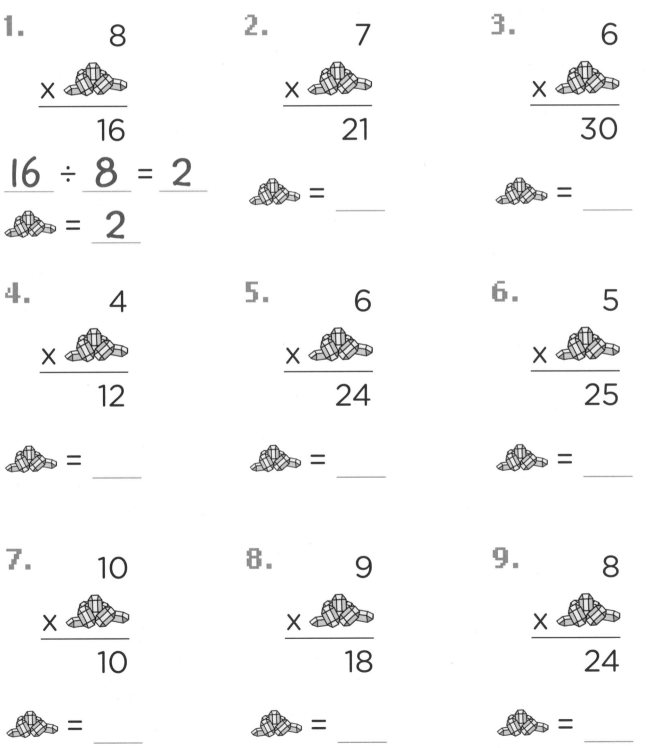

1.

$$8$$
$$\times \text{💎}$$
$$\overline{16}$$

$$16 \div 8 = 2$$

💎 = 2

2.

$$7$$
$$\times \text{💎}$$
$$\overline{21}$$

💎 = ___

3.

$$6$$
$$\times \text{💎}$$
$$\overline{30}$$

💎 = ___

4.

$$4$$
$$\times \text{💎}$$
$$\overline{12}$$

💎 = ___

5.

$$6$$
$$\times \text{💎}$$
$$\overline{24}$$

💎 = ___

6.

$$5$$
$$\times \text{💎}$$
$$\overline{25}$$

💎 = ___

7.

$$10$$
$$\times \text{💎}$$
$$\overline{10}$$

💎 = ___

8.

$$9$$
$$\times \text{💎}$$
$$\overline{18}$$

💎 = ___

9.

$$8$$
$$\times \text{💎}$$
$$\overline{24}$$

💎 = ___

MULTIPLICATION AND DIVISION
MYSTERY NUMBER

There is a number hidden behind these dragon eggs. Multiply the answer by the bottom number in the equation to find the mystery number. The first one is done for you.

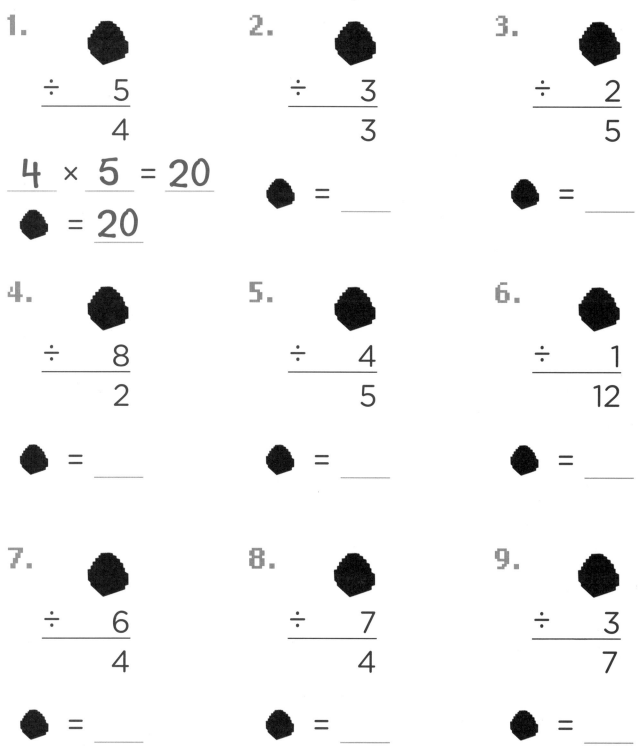

1.

$\div \quad 5$

$\quad\quad 4$

$\underline{4} \times \underline{5} = \underline{20}$

● $= \underline{20}$

2.

$\div \quad 3$

$\quad\quad 3$

● $= \underline{}$

3.

$\div \quad 2$

$\quad\quad 5$

● $= \underline{}$

4.

$\div \quad 8$

$\quad\quad 2$

● $= \underline{}$

5.

$\div \quad 4$

$\quad\quad 5$

● $= \underline{}$

6.

$\div \quad 1$

$\quad\quad 12$

● $= \underline{}$

7.

$\div \quad 6$

$\quad\quad 4$

● $= \underline{}$

8.

$\div \quad 7$

$\quad\quad 4$

● $= \underline{}$

9.

$\div \quad 3$

$\quad\quad 7$

● $= \underline{}$

MULTIPLICATION IN BASE 10

Multiply the numbers. Then fill in the place value chart. The first one is done for you.

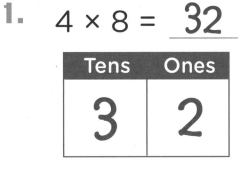

1. 4 × 8 = __32__

Tens	Ones
3	2

2. 6 × 5 = _____

Tens	Ones

3. 3 × 3 = _____

Tens	Ones

4. 4 × 6 = _____

Tens	Ones

5. 4 × 5 = _____

Tens	Ones

6. 2 × 8 = _____

Tens	Ones

7. 3 × 9 = _____

Tens	Ones

8. 4 × 9 = _____

Tens	Ones

MULTIPLICATION FACTS WITH BASE 10

Multiply the numbers. Then answer the questions.

1. $1 \times 10 = $ _____

2. $3 \times 10 = $ _____

3. $6 \times 10 = $ _____

4. $2 \times 10 = $ _____

5. $5 \times 10 = $ _____

6. $8 \times 10 = $ _____

7. $9 \times 10 = $ _____

8. $7 \times 10 = $ _____

9. $10 \times 10 = $ _____

10. $4 \times 10 = $ _____

Q: What pattern do you notice when you multiply a one-digit number by 10?

A: _____

Q: What pattern do you think would happen when you multiply a two-digit number by 10? Test your theory below.

A: _____

Example:

$10 \times 10 = $ _____

MULTIPLICATION BY GROUPING

Write the multiplication sentence that matches the picture. Then solve the equation. The first one is done for you.

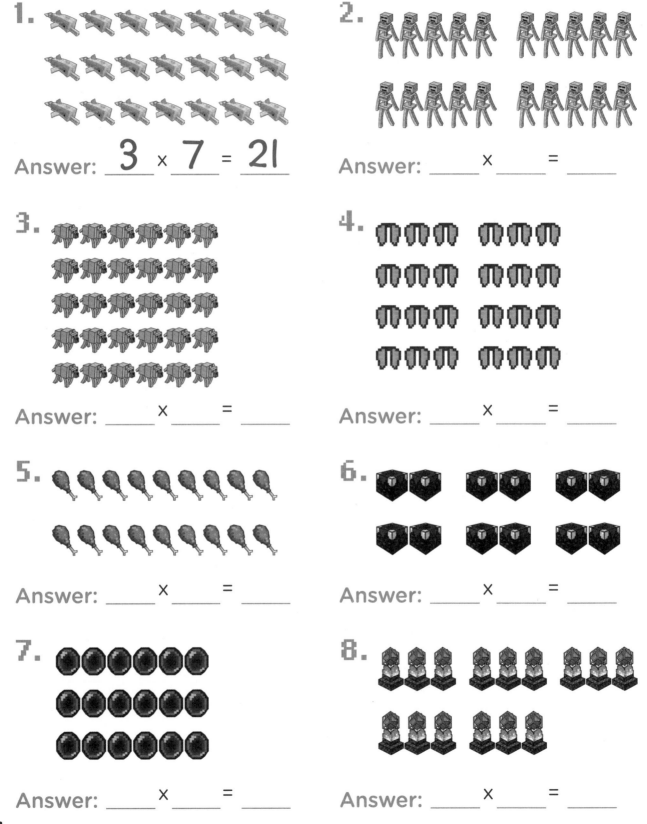

1.

Answer: ___3___ × ___7___ = __21__

2.

Answer: _____ × _____ = _____

3.

Answer: _____ × _____ = _____

4.

Answer: _____ × _____ = _____

5.

Answer: _____ × _____ = _____

6.

Answer: _____ × _____ = _____

7.

Answer: _____ × _____ = _____

8.

Answer: _____ × _____ = _____

MYSTERY MESSAGE
WITH MULTIPLICATION AND DIVISION

Multiply or divide. Then use the letters to fill in the blanks below and reveal the answer to Alex's riddle.

1. $20 \div 2 =$ _____ S

2. $9 \times 3 =$ _____ O

3. $15 \div 5 =$ _____ A

4. $6 \times 6 =$ _____ G

5. $18 \div 3 =$ _____ E

6. $5 \times 5 =$ _____ N

7. $35 \div 5 =$ _____ L

8. $8 \times 6 =$ _____ W

9. $90 \div 10 =$ _____ M

Q: It stays alive only if it stays cold. What is it?

Copy the letters from the answers above to solve the riddle.

___   ___ ___ ___ ___   ___ ___ ___ ___
 3   10 25 27 48   36 27 7   6   9

ENDERMAN'S GUIDE TO PLACE VALUE

Write the correct digit in the place value box.
The first one is done for you.

1. 726

ONES
6

2. 482

HUNDREDS

3. 629

TENS

4. 964

TENS

5. 371

HUNDREDS

6. 683

ONES

7. 392

TENS

8. 164

HUNDREDS

MATH FACTS CHALLENGE

Count by 7s and fill in the empty spaces to help
Alex craft a clock with the right ingredients.

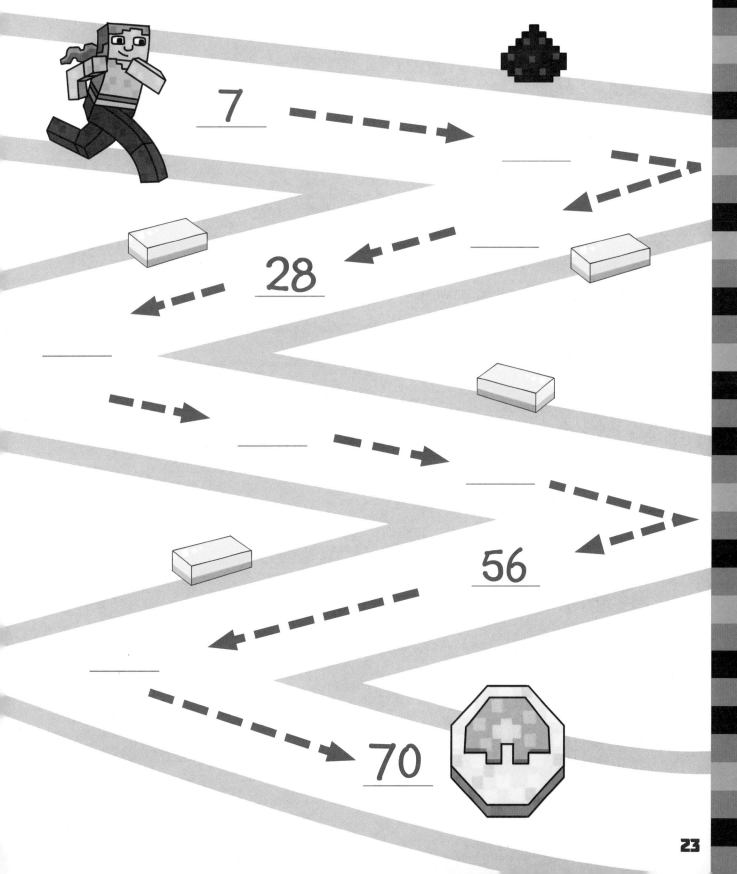

7

28

56

70

WORD PROBLEMS WITH MULTIPLICATION

Read the word problems. Use multiplication to find the answer.

Example: You mine 3 iron ore blocks every day for 3 days. How many blocks do you mine in all?

$$3 \times 3 = 9$$

Answer: **9 blocks**

1. There are 4 endermen and each one drops 5 ender pearls. How many ender pearls are dropped in all?

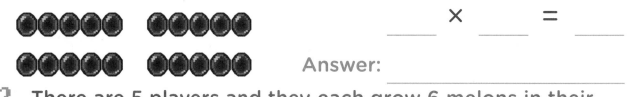

_____ × _____ = _____

Answer: _____

2. There are 5 players and they each grow 6 melons in their gardens. How many melons do they grow all together?

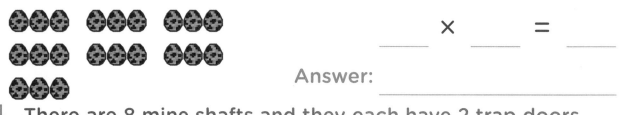

_____ × _____ = _____

Answer: _____

3. There are 7 turtles and they each spawn 3 turtle eggs. How many turtle eggs do they spawn in all?

_____ × _____ = _____

Answer: _____

4. There are 8 mine shafts and they each have 2 trap doors hidden in them. How many trap doors are there in all?

_____ × _____ = _____

Answer: _____

WORD PROBLEMS WITH DIVISION

Read the word problems. Use division to find the answer.

Example: The village librarian offered to give 18 of his books to Alex and Steve. They each got the same number of books. How many books did each player get?

$$18 \div 2 = 9$$

Answer: __9 books__

1. You need 20 lava blocks to build a lava field. How many lava blocks does each player need if there are 5 players working together to build it?

___ $\div$ ___ = ___

Answer: _____

2. There are 4 bees in a hive that produces a total of 12 bottles of honey. If each bee produces the same amount, how much honey does each bee produce?

___ $\div$ ___ = ___

Answer: _____

3. Alex has 24 carrots and 3 pigs to tame. How many carrots can each pig get?

___ $\div$ ___ = ___

Answer: _____

4. There are 15 torches and 3 mine shafts. How many torches can be placed in each mine shaft?

___ $\div$ ___ = ___

Answer: _____

REGROUPING IN BASE 10: MULTIPLICATION

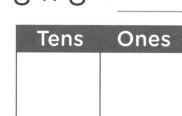

Multiply the numbers. Then fill in the place value chart. The first one is done for you.

1. 6 × 7 = <u>42</u>

Tens	Ones
4	2

2. 8 × 8 = _____

Tens	Ones

3. 8 × 4 = _____

Tens	Ones

4. 5 × 8 = _____

Tens	Ones

5. 5 × 6 = _____

Tens	Ones

6. 6 × 8 = _____

Tens	Ones

7. 6 × 4 = _____

Tens	Ones

8. 7 × 3 = _____

Tens	Ones

REGROUPING IN BASE 10: DIVISION

Divide the numbers. Then fill in the place value chart.
The first one is done for you.

1. 20 ÷ 2 = __10__

Tens	Ones
1	0

2. 81 ÷ 9 = _____

Tens	Ones

3. 33 ÷ 3 = _____

Tens	Ones

4. 15 ÷ 1 = _____

Tens	Ones

5. 20 ÷ 4 = _____

Tens	Ones

6. 28 ÷ 2 = _____

Tens	Ones

7. 50 ÷ 2 = _____

Tens	Ones

8. 36 ÷ 6 = _____

Tens	Ones

MULTIPLICATION MATH FACTS WITH 2

Multiply the numbers. Then answer the question.

1. $3 \times 2 =$ _____

2. $5 \times 2 =$ _____

3. $7 \times 2 =$ _____

4. $10 \times 2 =$ _____

5. $8 \times 2 =$ _____

6. $9 \times 2 =$ _____

7. $11 \times 2 =$ _____

8. $6 \times 2 =$ _____

9. $12 \times 2 =$ _____

10. $2 \times 2 =$ _____

11. $2 \times 3 =$ _____

12. $2 \times 8 =$ _____

13. $2 \times 7 =$ _____

14. $11 \times 2 =$ _____

15. $2 \times 5 =$ _____

Q: Circle all of the products that are even numbers. What do you notice when you multiply a number by 2?

A: _____

MULTIPLICATION MATH FACTS WITH 5

Multiply the numbers. Then answer the questions.

1. 3 × 5 = _____

2. 8 × 5 = _____

3. 7 × 5 = _____

4. 10 × 5 = _____

5. 9 × 5 = _____

6. 6 × 5 = _____

7. 11 × 5 = _____

8. 4 × 5 = _____

9. 1 × 5 = _____

10. 2 × 5 = _____

11. 5 × 3 = _____

12. 5 × 8 = _____

13. 5 × 7 = _____

14. 5 × 11 = _____

15. 5 × 5 = _____

Q: Circle all of the products that end in 5. What do you notice when you multiply an odd number by 5?

A: _____

Q: Put a square around all of the products that end in 0. What do you notice when you multiply an even number by 5?

A: _____

BABY ZOMBIE'S GUIDE TO PLACE VALUE

Use the number on each baby zombie to fill in the place value chart.

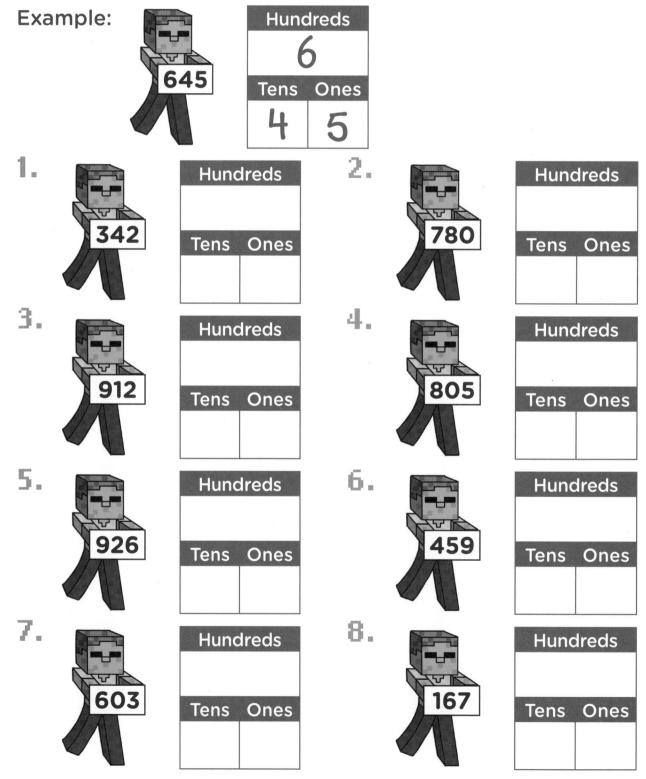

Example:

645

Hundreds	
6	
Tens	Ones
4	5

1. **342**

Hundreds	
Tens	Ones

2. **780**

Hundreds	
Tens	Ones

3. **912**

Hundreds	
Tens	Ones

4. **805**

Hundreds	
Tens	Ones

5. **926**

Hundreds	
Tens	Ones

6. **459**

Hundreds	
Tens	Ones

7. **603**

Hundreds	
Tens	Ones

8. **167**

Hundreds	
Tens	Ones

MATH FACTS CHALLENGE

Count by 8s and fill in the empty spaces to help Steve get his shield before the blaze hits him with fireballs.

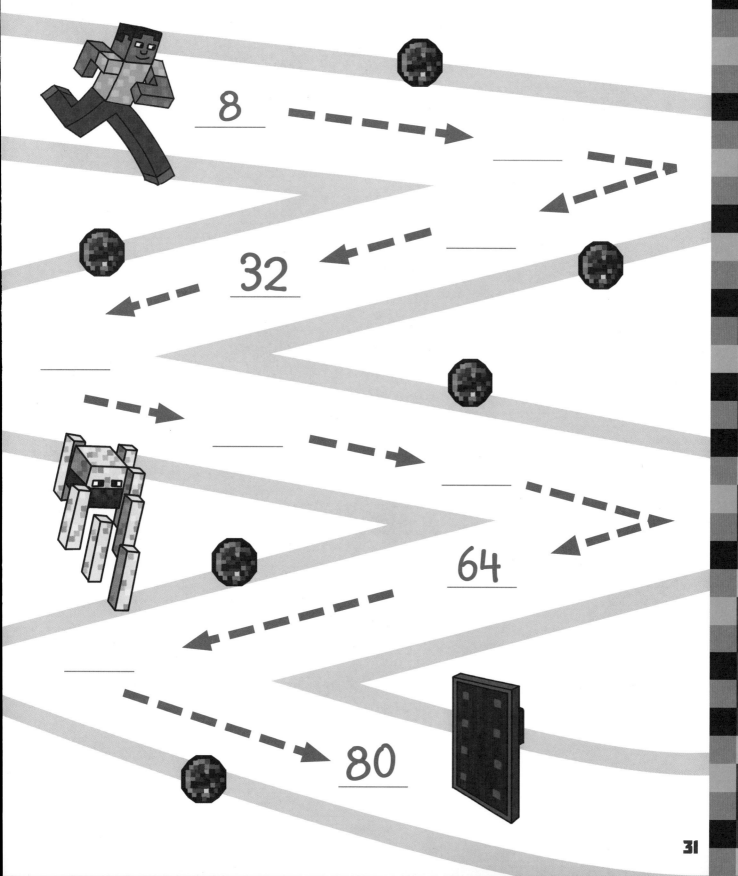

8

32

64

80

MULTIPLICATION AND DIVISION
MYSTERY NUMBER

There is a number hidden behind these anvils. Divide the product by the known number to find the mystery number. The first one is done for you.

1.
$$\begin{array}{r} 8 \\ \times \quad \blacksquare \\ \hline 48 \end{array}$$

$$48 \div 8 = 6$$

$\blacksquare = 6$

2.
$$\begin{array}{r} 5 \\ \times \quad \blacksquare \\ \hline 25 \end{array}$$

$\blacksquare = \underline{\quad}$

3.
$$\begin{array}{r} 8 \\ \times \quad \blacksquare \\ \hline 64 \end{array}$$

$\blacksquare = \underline{\quad}$

4.
$$\begin{array}{r} 7 \\ \times \quad \blacksquare \\ \hline 21 \end{array}$$

$\blacksquare = \underline{\quad}$

5.
$$\begin{array}{r} 10 \\ \times \quad \blacksquare \\ \hline 40 \end{array}$$

$\blacksquare = \underline{\quad}$

6.
$$\begin{array}{r} 9 \\ \times \quad \blacksquare \\ \hline 63 \end{array}$$

$\blacksquare = \underline{\quad}$

7.
$$\begin{array}{r} 6 \\ \times \quad \blacksquare \\ \hline 36 \end{array}$$

$\blacksquare = \underline{\quad}$

8.
$$\begin{array}{r} 4 \\ \times \quad \blacksquare \\ \hline 36 \end{array}$$

$\blacksquare = \underline{\quad}$

9.
$$\begin{array}{r} 5 \\ \times \quad \blacksquare \\ \hline 55 \end{array}$$

$\blacksquare = \underline{\quad}$

MYSTERY MESSAGE
WITH MULTIPLICATION AND DIVISION

Use answers 1-8 from page 32 to fill in the chart. Then use the letters to fill in the answer and solve the riddle.

QUESTION	ANSWER	LETTER
1.		M
2.		A
3.		S
4.		L
5.		C
6.		I
7.		U
8.		E

Q: What has six faces and is very bouncy?

Copy the letters from the chart to solve the riddle.

___   ___ ___ ___ ___ ___
5   8   3   7   6   9

MULTIPLICATION IN BASE 10

Multiply the numbers. Then draw a line to the correct place value description. The first one is done for you.

1. 7 × 5 = __35__

2. 8 × 3 = _____

3. 4 × 5 = _____

4. 5 × 9 = _____

5. 7 × 9 = _____

6. 7 × 8 = _____

7. 4 × 3 = _____

8. 7 × 3 = _____

ONES
0

TENS
3

TENS
6

ONES
4

TENS
5

ONES
1

TENS
4

ONES
2

DIVISION IN BASE 10

Divide the numbers. Then draw a line to the correct place value description. The first one is done for you.

1. $27 \div 9 = \underline{\quad 3 \quad}$

2. $45 \div 5 = \underline{\qquad}$

3. $60 \div 2 = \underline{\qquad}$

4. $80 \div 2 = \underline{\qquad}$

5. $56 \div 7 = \underline{\qquad}$

6. $10 \div 1 = \underline{\qquad}$

7. $24 \div 6 = \underline{\qquad}$

8. $40 \div 8 = \underline{\qquad}$

ONES
9

TENS
4

TENS
1

ONES
3

ONES
5

ONES
8

TENS
3

ONES
4

MULTIPLICATION MATH FACTS

Multiply the numbers. Draw a line from column A to the same answer in column B. Then answer the question. The first one is done for you.

A

1. $3 \times 9 =$ **27**
2. $5 \times 6 =$ _____
3. $7 \times 9 =$ _____
4. $10 \times 4 =$ _____
5. $6 \times 4 =$ _____
6. $9 \times 2 =$ _____
7. $11 \times 3 =$ _____
8. $6 \times 2 =$ _____

B

9. $9 \times 7 =$ _____
10. $4 \times 6 =$ _____
11. $3 \times 11 =$ _____
12. $6 \times 5 =$ _____
13. $9 \times 3 =$ **27**
14. $4 \times 10 =$ _____
15. $2 \times 6 =$ _____
16. $2 \times 9 =$ _____

Q: What do you notice about the order of numbers in a multiplication problem?

A:_____

MULTIPLICATION BY GROUPING

Write the multiplication sentence that matches the picture. Then solve the equation. The first one is done for you.

1.

Answer: $6 \times 2 = 12$

2.

Answer: _____ × _____ = _____

3.

Answer: _____ × _____ = _____

4.

Answer: _____ × _____ = _____

5.

Answer: _____ × _____ = _____

6.

Answer: _____ × _____ = _____

7.

Answer: _____ × _____ = _____

8.

Answer: _____ × _____ = _____

ROUNDING IN BASE 10

Multiply the numbers. Then round the number up or down to the nearest ten. The first one is done for you.

Hint: Numbers ending in 0, 1, 2, 3, and 4 round *down*. Numbers ending in 5, 6, 7, 8, and 9 round *up*.

Multiply	Solve it!	Round it!
1. 6 × 6 =	_____	_____
2. 8 × 6 =	_____	_____
3. 3 × 9 =	_____	_____
4. 2 × 6 =	_____	_____
5. 7 × 2 =	_____	_____
6. 5 × 7 =	_____	_____
7. 10 × 2 =	_____	_____
8. 9 × 4 =	_____	_____
9. 4 × 7 =	_____	_____
10. 5 × 4 =	_____	_____

MATH FACTS CHALLENGE

Find the pattern and fill in the empty spaces to help Alex escape the teleporting Enderman.

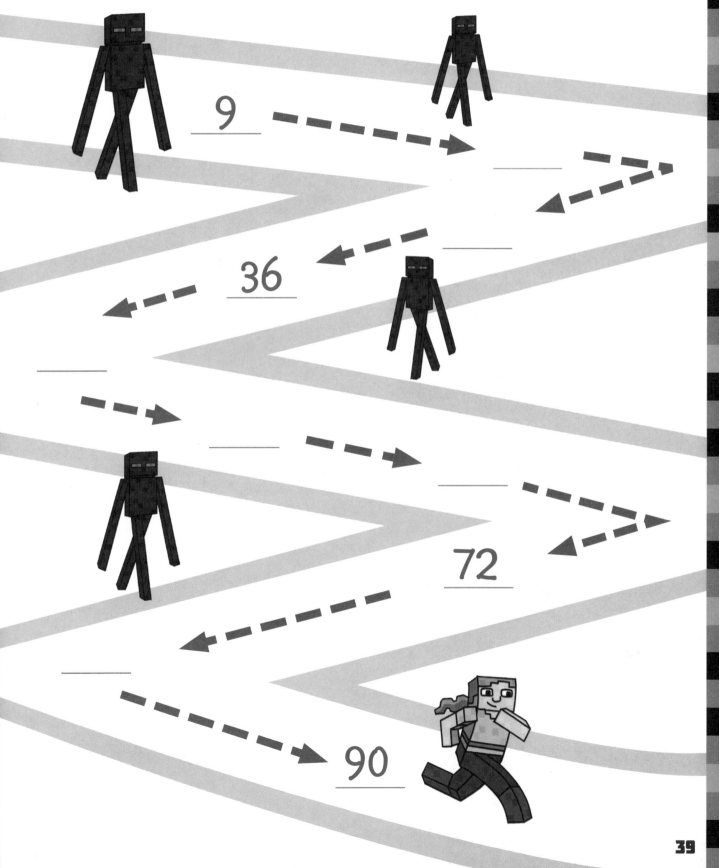

9

___

___

36

___

___

72

___

90

WORD PROBLEMS WITH MULTIPLICATION

Read the word problems. Use multiplication to find the answer.

Example: Steve plants 4 rows of 6 potatoes. How many potatoes does Steve plant in all?

$4 \times 6 = 24$

Answer: 24 potatoes

1. Alex crafts 5 diamond swords each day for a week. How many diamond swords does she have at the end of 7 days?

_____ $\times$ _____ = _____

Answer: _____

2. A mob blows up 6 pigs every time it explodes. How many pigs blow up when 4 mobs explode?

_____ $\times$ _____ = _____

Answer: _____

3. You need 4 blocks of wood to make one plank. How blocks of wood do you need to make 7 planks?

_____ $\times$ _____ = _____

Answer: _____

4. Alex needs 3 TNT blocks to blow up each silverfish block. How many TNT blocks does she need to destroy 6 silverfish blocks?

_____ $\times$ _____ = _____

Answer: _____

WORD PROBLEMS WITH DIVISION

Read the word problems. Use division to find the answer.

Example: Steve has 27 stone blocks. Each wall needs 9 stone blocks. How many walls can Steve build?

$$27 \div 9 = 3$$

Answer: **3 walls**

1. The librarian has 30 books and each shelf hold 6 books. How many shelves does the librarian need for all the books?

___ ÷ ___ = ___

Answer: _____

2. Alex collects 40 apples from 4 trees. If each tree had the same amount of apples, how many apples came from each tree?

___ ÷ ___ = ___

Answer: _____

3. Alex and Steve find a stash of 18 arrows. How many arrows can they have if they split them evenly?

___ ÷ ___ = ___

Answer: _____

4. Steve has 24 buckets of water and 6 rows of plants. How many buckets of water can he pour on each row of plants?

___ ÷ ___ = ___

Answer: _____

EXPANDED FORM IN BASE 10

Write the number on each shulker in expanded form in the space provided.

Example:  215   Answer:

200 + 10 + 5

1. 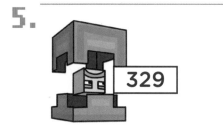 391

2.  756

3. 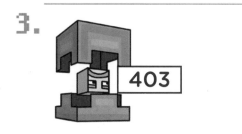 403

4. 186

5. 329

6. 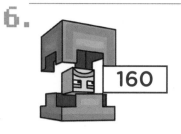 160

7. 486

8. 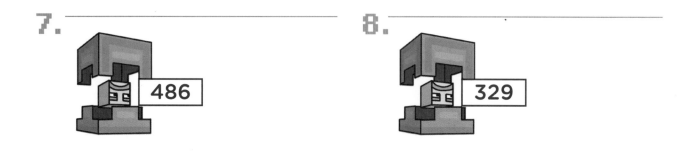 329

EXPANDED FORM IN BASE 10

Write the number on each Enderman in expanded form in the space provided.

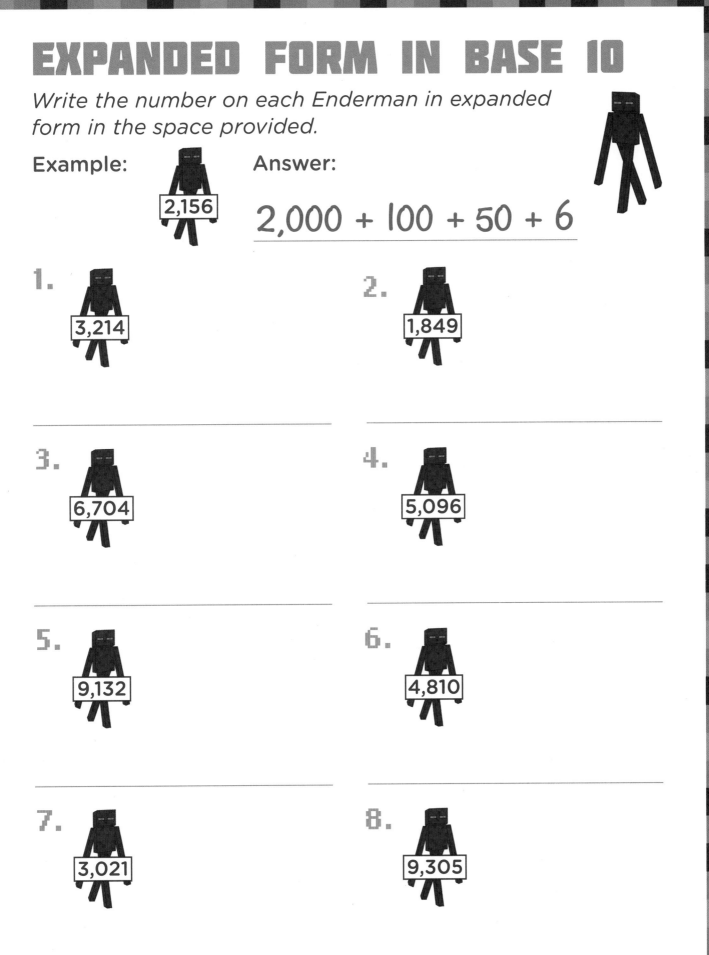

Example:

2,156

Answer:

2,000 + 100 + 50 + 6

1.

3,214

2.

1,849

3.

6,704

4.

5,096

5.

9,132

6.

4,810

7.

3,021

8.

9,305

MULTIPLICATION MATH FACTS WITH 9

Multiply the numbers.

1. 3 × 9 = _____

2. 5 × 9 = _____

3. 7 × 9 = _____

4. 8 × 9 = _____

5. 4 × 9 = _____

6. 9 × 1 = _____

7. 9 × 2 = _____

8. 6 × 9 = _____

9. 4 × 9 = _____

10. 9 × 3 = _____

11. 9 × 6 = _____

12. 1 × 9 = _____

13. 9 × 4 = _____

14. 9 × 9 = _____

15. 9 × 2 = _____

MYSTERY MESSAGE WITH DIVISION

Divide. Then use the letters to fill in the blanks below and reveal the answer to Steve's riddle.

1. 81 ÷ 9 = _____ <u>M</u>

2. 42 ÷ 7 = _____ <u>T</u>

3. 50 ÷ 10 = _____ <u>A</u>

4. 36 ÷ 9 = _____ <u>O</u>

5. 24 ÷ 3 = _____ <u>I</u>

6. 80 ÷ 8 = _____ <u>G</u>

7. 49 ÷ 7 = _____ <u>E</u>

8. 18 ÷ 6 = _____ <u>R</u>

9. 99 ÷ 9 = _____ <u>V</u>

Q: How do you get a mob to scare itself?

Copy the letters from the answers above to solve the riddle.

___ ___ ___ ___   ___ ___ ___
10   8   11   7   8   6   5

___ ___ ___ ___ ___ ___
 9   8   3   3   4   3

SNOW GOLEM'S GUIDE TO PLACE VALUE

Use the chart on the right to write the number on the snow golem.

Example:

`145`

Hundreds	
1	
Tens	Ones
4	5

1.

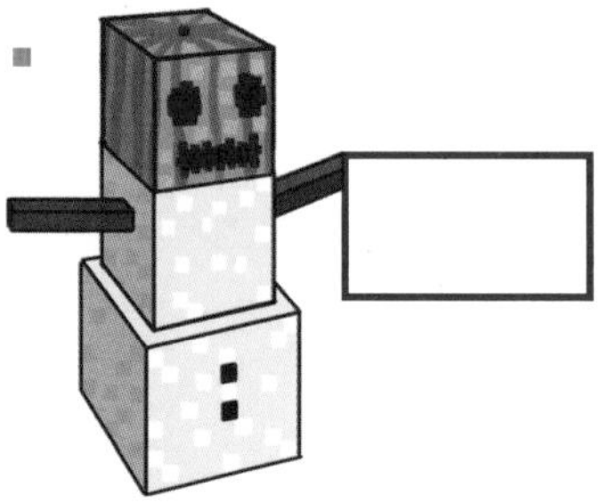

Hundreds	
6	
Tens	Ones
9	4

2.

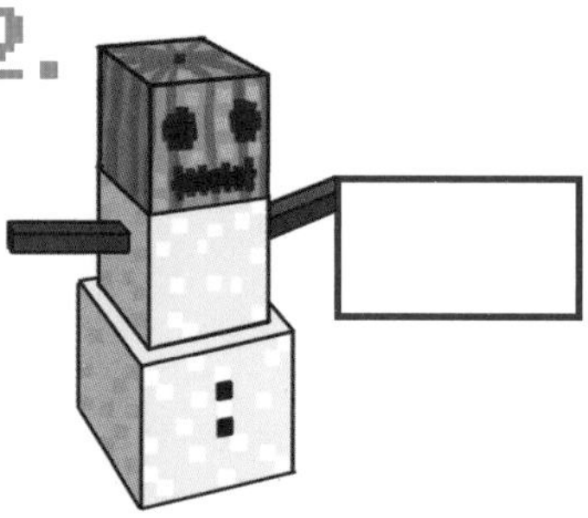

Hundreds	
0	
Tens	Ones
3	7

3.

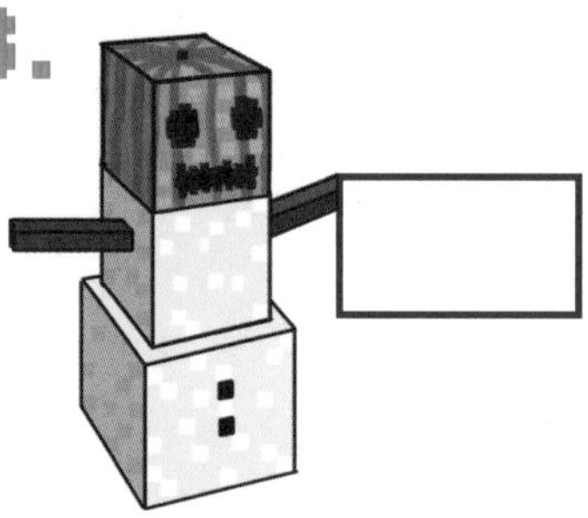

Hundreds	
2	
Tens	Ones
0	1

4.

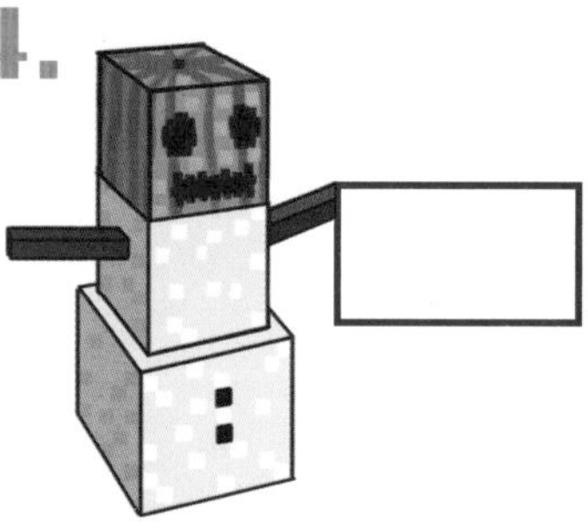

Hundreds	
8	
Tens	Ones
3	0

5.

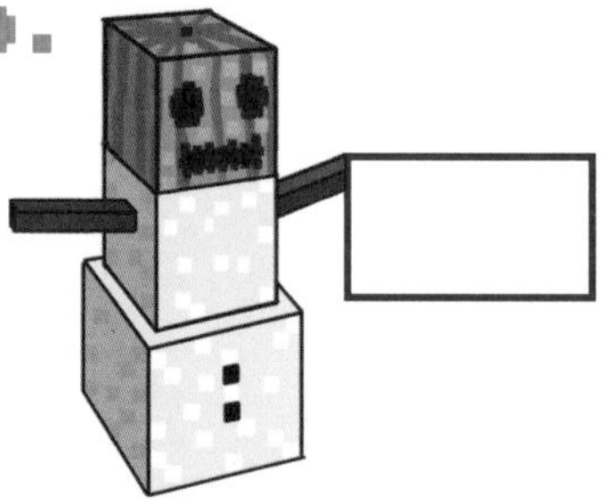

Hundreds	
4	
Tens	Ones
2	9

6.

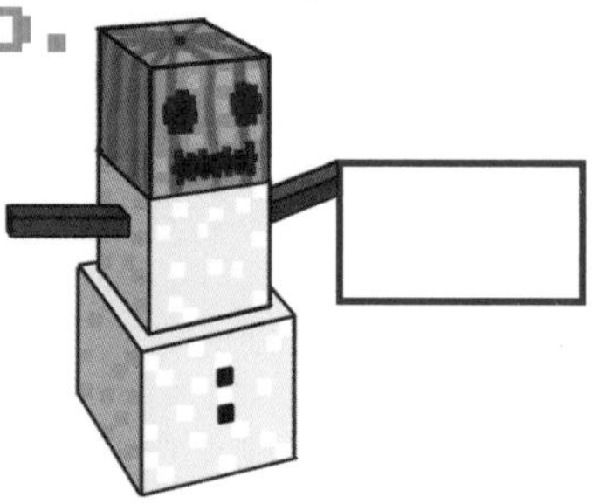

Hundreds	
5	
Tens	Ones
0	4

7.

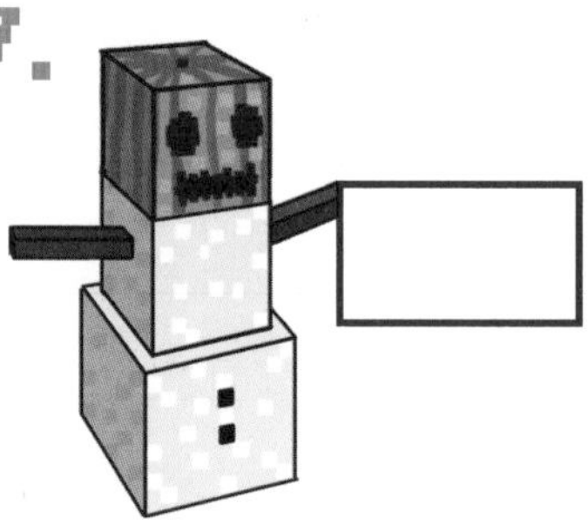

Hundreds	
6	
Tens	Ones
7	0

8.

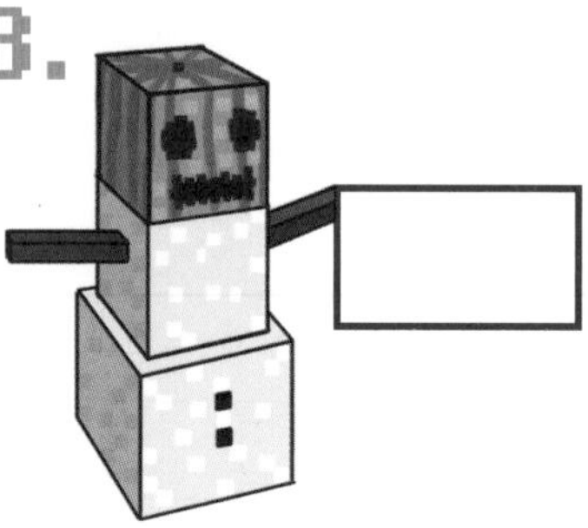

Hundreds	
9	
Tens	Ones
3	4

MATH FACTS CHALLENGE

Count by 4s and fill in the empty spaces to help Steve craft his diamond armor.

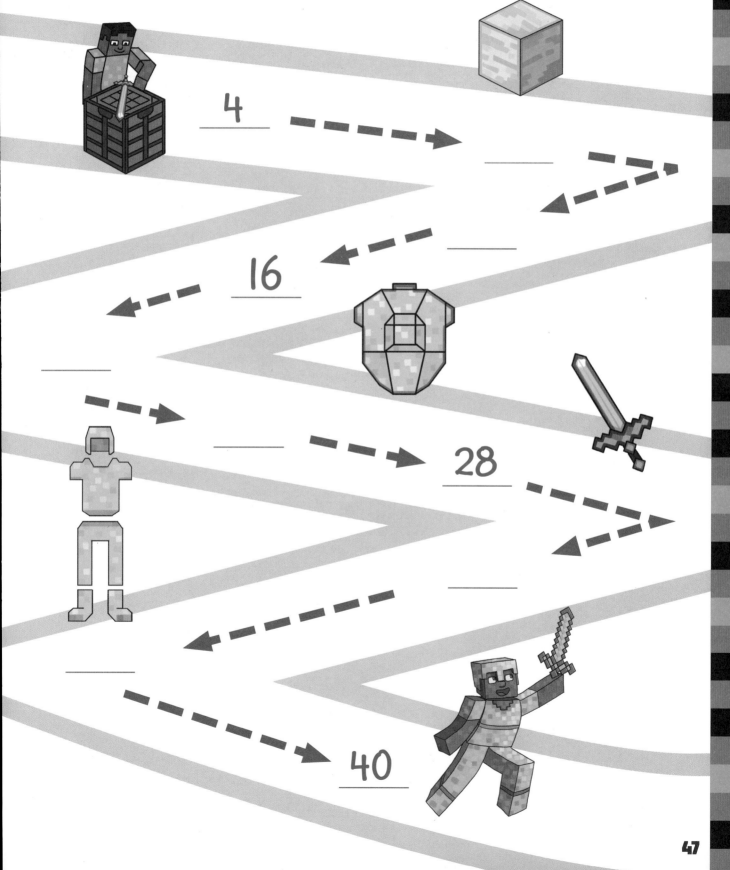

4 ___ ___

___

16 ___

___

___ 28 ___

___

___

40

MULTIPLICATION AND DIVISION
MYSTERY NUMBER

There is a number hidden behind these emeralds. Rewrite the equation as a division problem to discover the mystery number. The first one is done for you.

	Rewrite the Equation	Solve It
1. 7 ×  = 63	63 ÷ 7 = 	 = 9
2. 8 ×  = 24	____ ÷ ____ = 	 = ____
3. 6 ×  = 36	____ ÷ ____ = 	 = ____
4. 2 ×  = 20	____ ÷ ____ = 	 = ____
5. 9 ×  = 54	____ ÷ ____ = 	 = ____
6. 5 ×  = 35	____ ÷ ____ = 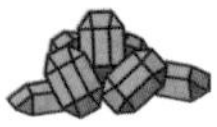	 = ____
7. 4 ×  = 24	____ ÷ ____ = 	 = ____
8. 9 ×  = 27	____ ÷ ____ = 	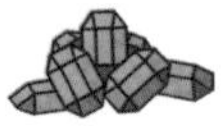 = ____
9. 5 ×  = 25	____ ÷ ____ = 	 = ____

MULTIPLICATION AND DIVISION
MYSTERY NUMBER

There is a number hidden behind these experience orbs. Rewrite the equation as a multiplication problem to discover the mystery number. The first one is done for you.

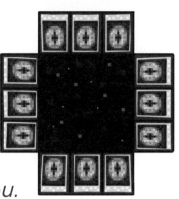

	Rewrite the Equation	**Solve It**

1. ⬡ ÷ 3 = 6   <u>6</u> × <u>3</u> = ⬡   ⬡ = <u>18</u>

2. ⬡ ÷ 7 = 8   ___ × ___ = ⬡   ⬡ = ___

3. ⬡ ÷ 5 = 6   ___ × ___ = ⬡   ⬡ = ___

4. ⬡ ÷ 10 = 4   ___ × ___ = ⬡   ⬡ = ___

5. ⬡ ÷ 5 = 9   ___ × ___ = ⬡   ⬡ = ___

6. ⬡ ÷ 4 = 6   ___ × ___ = ⬡   ⬡ = ___

7. ⬡ ÷ 8 = 8   ___ × ___ = ⬡   ⬡ = ___

8. ⬡ ÷ 10 = 5   ___ × ___ = ⬡   ⬡ = ___

9. ⬡ ÷ 3 = 9   ___ × ___ = ⬡   ⬡ = ___

MULTIPLICATION IN BASE 10

Multiply the numbers. Then fill in the place value chart. The first one is done for you.

1. 13 × 10 = <u>130</u>

Hundreds	Tens	Ones
1	3	0

2. 54 × 10 = ____

Hundreds	Tens	Ones

3. 43 × 10 = ____

Hundreds	Tens	Ones

4. 92 × 10 = ____

Hundreds	Tens	Ones

5. 80 × 10 = ____

Hundreds	Tens	Ones

6. 34 × 10 = ____

Hundreds	Tens	Ones

7. 26 × 10 = ____

Hundreds	Tens	Ones

8. 31 × 10 = ____

Hundreds	Tens	Ones

Q: What do you notice about how a number changes when you multiply by 10?

A: _____

DIVISION IN BASE 10

Divide the numbers. Then round the number up or down to the nearest ten. The first one is done for you.

Hint: Numbers 0, 1, 2, 3, and 4 round *down*. Numbers 5, 6, 7, 8, and 9 round *up*.

Divide	Solve it!	Round it!
1. 240 ÷ 10 =	24	20
2. 690 ÷ 10 =	_____	_____
3. 430 ÷ 10 =	_____	_____
4. 120 ÷ 10 =	_____	_____
5. 320 ÷ 10 =	_____	_____
6. 470 ÷ 10 =	_____	_____
7. 270 ÷ 10 =	_____	_____
8. 180 ÷ 10 =	_____	_____

DIVISION BY GROUPING

The villagers want to share this pie equally. Use the image of the pie to help you answer the questions.

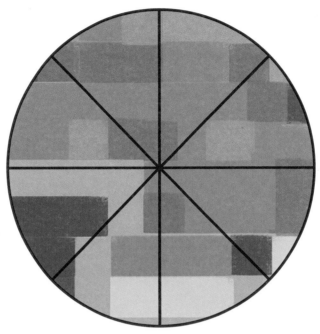

1. How many slices of this pie could 2 villagers have?

   _____

2. How many slices of pie could 4 villagers have?

   _____

3. How many slices of pie could 8 villagers have?

   _____

4. If you wanted to feed 16 villagers, what could you do?

   _____

5. If you wanted to feed 24 villagers, what could you do?

   _____

MYSTERY MESSAGE
WITH MULTIPLICATION AND DIVISION

Multiply or divide. Then use the letters to fill in the blanks below and reveal the answer to Alex's riddle.

1. $72 \div 8 =$ _____ __N__

2. $7 \times 4 =$ _____ __U__

3. $45 \div 9 =$ _____ __D__

4. $6 \times 5 =$ _____ __I__

5. $63 \div 9 =$ _____ __E__

6. $8 \times 4 =$ _____ __W__

7. $42 \div 7 =$ _____ __O__

8. $9 \times 3 =$ _____ __P__

9. $56 \div 7 =$ _____ __S__

Q: How do you make a frowning mob smile?

Copy the letters from the answers above to solve the riddle.

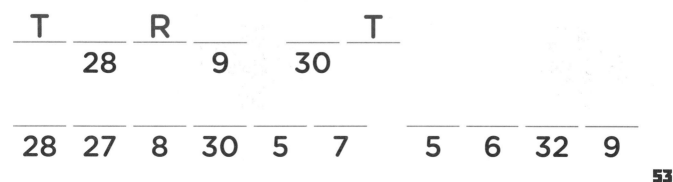

WITHER'S GUIDE TO PLACE VALUE

Use the chart on the right to write the number on the wither. Don't forget the comma!

Example:

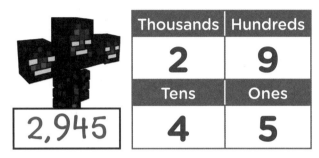

Thousands	Hundreds
2	9
Tens	**Ones**
4	5

2,945

1.

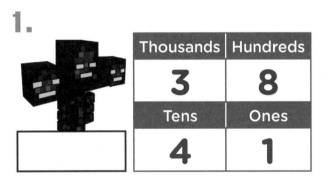

Thousands	Hundreds
3	8
Tens	**Ones**
4	1

2.

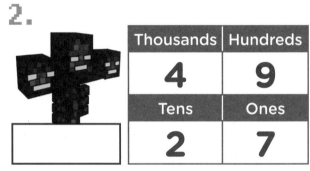

Thousands	Hundreds
4	9
Tens	**Ones**
2	7

3.

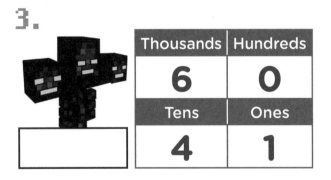

Thousands	Hundreds
6	0
Tens	**Ones**
4	1

4.

Thousands	Hundreds
8	7
Tens	**Ones**
0	5

5.

Thousands	Hundreds
0	3
Tens	**Ones**
4	2

6.

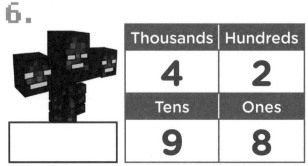

Thousands	Hundreds
4	2
Tens	**Ones**
9	8

MATH FACTS CHALLENGE

Find the pattern and fill in the empty spaces to help Steve get to the end portal before the Ender dragon gets him.

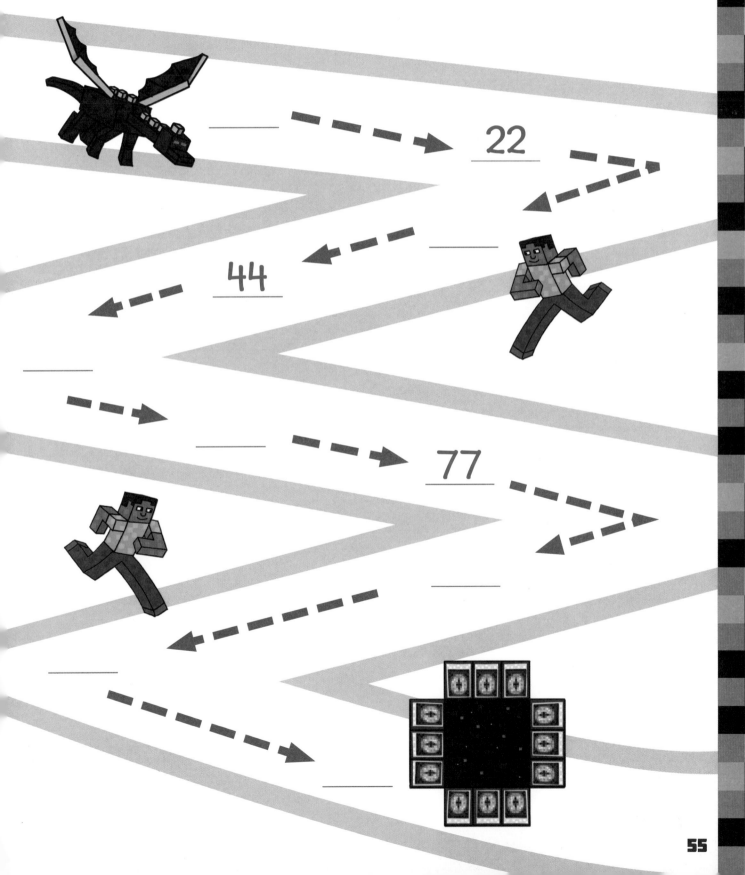

MULTIPLICATION AND DIVISION
MYSTERY NUMBER

There is a number hidden behind these beacons. Divide the product by the known number to find the mystery number. The first one is done for you.

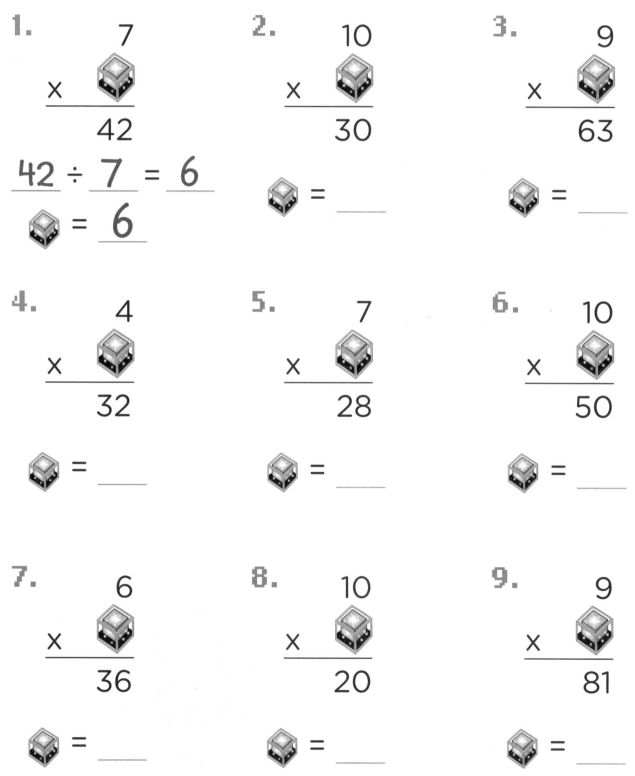

1.
$$\begin{array}{r} 7 \\ \times \\ \hline 42 \end{array}$$

$42 \div 7 = 6$

■ = 6

2.
$$\begin{array}{r} 10 \\ \times \\ \hline 30 \end{array}$$

■ = ___

3.
$$\begin{array}{r} 9 \\ \times \\ \hline 63 \end{array}$$

■ = ___

4.
$$\begin{array}{r} 4 \\ \times \\ \hline 32 \end{array}$$

■ = ___

5.
$$\begin{array}{r} 7 \\ \times \\ \hline 28 \end{array}$$

■ = ___

6.
$$\begin{array}{r} 10 \\ \times \\ \hline 50 \end{array}$$

■ = ___

7.
$$\begin{array}{r} 6 \\ \times \\ \hline 36 \end{array}$$

■ = ___

8.
$$\begin{array}{r} 10 \\ \times \\ \hline 20 \end{array}$$

■ = ___

9.
$$\begin{array}{r} 9 \\ \times \\ \hline 81 \end{array}$$

■ = ___

MYSTERY MESSAGE
WITH MULTIPLICATION AND DIVISION

Use the answers you found on page 56 to fill in the chart. Then use the letters to fill in the answer and solve the riddle.

QUESTION	ANSWER	LETTER
2.		T
3.		F
4.		O
5.		A
6.		N
7.		C
8.		I
9.		P

Q: This is a coat that will always be wet when you put it on. What is it?

 4   6   8   4   3   8   7

 9   4   2   5   3

WORD PROBLEMS WITH MULTIPLICATION

Use the information below to write a multiplication word problem. Then solve it.

Example: 4 players, 3 axes

$$\underline{\quad 4 \quad} \times \underline{\quad 3 \quad} = \underline{\quad 12 \quad}$$

Q: <u>There are 4 players and each one has 3 swords. How many swords do they have all together?</u>

A: <u>They have 12 swords.</u>

1. 5 skeletons, 6 arrows

$$\underline{\qquad} \times \underline{\qquad} = \underline{\qquad}$$

Q: _____

_____

A: _____

2. 3 ocelots, 6 fish

$$\underline{\qquad} \times \underline{\qquad} = \underline{\qquad}$$

Q: _____

_____

A: _____

3. 6 witches, 4 potions

$$\underline{\qquad} \times \underline{\qquad} = \underline{\qquad}$$

Q: _____

_____

A: _____

WORD PROBLEMS WITH DIVISION

Use the information below to write a division word problem. Then solve it.

Example: 5 fishing poles, 30 fish

$$\underline{30} \div \underline{5} = \underline{6}$$

Q: Steve uses 5 fishing poles to catch 30 fish. If he catches the same number of fish with each pole, how many fish does each pole catch?

A: Each pole catches 6 fish.

1. 4 ender dragons, 28 dragon eggs

   ____ ÷ ____ = ____

   Q: _____

   _____

   A: _____

2. 6 gold ingots, 18 golden swords

   ____ ÷ ____ = ____

   Q: _____

   _____

   A: _____

3. 4 chickens, 12 eggs

   ____ ÷ ____ = ____

   Q: _____

   _____

   A: _____

ANSWER KEY

Page 4

1. 8
2. 10
3. 6
4. 15

Page 5

1. 27
2. 24
3. 50
4. 42
5. 35
6. 22
7. 30
8. 72

Jiffy Cube

Page 6

1. 800 + 00 + 1
2. 100 + 60 + 7
3. 400 + 50 + 0
4. 800 + 30 + 4
5. 300 + 20 + 6
6. 700 + 30 + 5

Page 7

5, 10, 15, 20, 25, 30,
35, 40, 45, 50, 55

Page 8

1. 4
2. 5
3. 2
4. 6
5. 3
6. 0

Page 9

1. 7
2. 8
3. 6
4. 5
5. 8
6. 9

Page 10

1. 56; 5 tens 6 ones
2. 35; 3 tens, 5 ones
3. 24; 2 tens, 4 ones
4. 63; 6 tens, 3 ones
5. 64; 6 tens, 4 ones
6. 18; 1 ten, 8 ones
7. 50; 5 tens, 0 ones
8. 27; 2 tens, 7 ones

Page 11

1. 6; 10
2. 8; 10
3. 3; 0
4. 2; 0
5. 7; 10
6. 6; 10
7. 2; 0
8. 4; 0

Page 12

1. 12
2. 24
3. 15
4. 16
5. 21
6. 35

Page 13

1. 2
2. 7
3. 10
4. 5
5. 9
6. 3
7. 7
8. 4

Guardians

Page 14

1. 9
2. 6
3. 0
4. 3
5. 8
6. 5
7. 0
8. 1

Page 15

6, 12, 18, 24, 30, 36,
42, 48, 54, 60, 66

Page 16

1. 2
2. 3
3. 5
4. 3
5. 4
6. 5
7. 1
8. 2
9. 3

Page 17

1. 20
2. 9
3. 10
4. 16
5. 20
6. 12
7. 24
8. 28
9. 21

Page 18

1. 32; 3 tens, 2 ones
2. 30; 3 tens, 0 ones
3. 9; 0 tens, 9 ones
4. 24; 2 tens, 4 ones
5. 20; 2 tens, 0 ones
6. 16; 1 ten, 6 ones
7. 27; 2 tens, 7 ones
8. 36; 3 tens, 6 ones

Page 19

1. 10
2. 30
3. 60
4. 20
5. 50
6. 80
7. 90
8. 70
9. 100
10. 40

You add a 0 to the end of the number and get a two-digit number.

You add a 0 to the end of the number and get a three-digit number. Examples: 100, 200, 300

Page 20

1. 21
2. 20
3. 30
4. 24
5. 18
6. 12
7. 18
8. 15

Page 21

1. 10
2. 27
3. 3
4. 36
5. 6
6. 25
7. 7
8. 48
9. *A snow golem*

Page 22

1. 6
2. 4
3. 2
4. 6
5. 3
6. 3
7. 9
8. 1

Page 23

7, 14, 21, 28, 35, 42, 49, 56, 63, 70

Page 24

1. 20 ender pearls
2. 30 melons
3. 21 turtle eggs
4. 16 trap doors

Page 25

1. 4 lava blocks
2. 3 honey bottles
3. 8 carrots
4. 5 torches

Page 26

1. 42; 4 tens, 2 ones
2. 64; 6 tens, 4 ones
3. 32; 3 tens, 2 ones
4. 40; 4 tens, 0 ones
5. 30; 3 tens, 0 ones
6. 48; 4 tens, 8 ones
7. 24; 2 tens, 4 ones
8. 21; 2 tens, 1 one

Page 27

1. 10; 1 ten, 0 ones
2. 9; 0 tens, 9 ones
3. 11; 1 ten, 1 one
4. 15; 1 ten, 5 ones
5. 5; 0 tens, 5 ones
6. 14; 1 ten, 4 ones
7. 25; 2 tens, 5 ones
8. 6; 0 tens, 6 ones

Page 28

1. 6
2. 10
3. 14
4. 20
5. 16
6. 18
7. 22
8. 12
9. 24
10. 4
11. 6
12. 16
13. 14
14. 22
15. 10

When you multiply a number by 2, the product is always even.

Page 29

1. 15
2. 40
3. 35
4. 50
5. 45
6. 30
7. 55
8. 20
9. 5
10. 10
11. 15
12. 40
13. 35
14. 55
15. 25

When you multiply an odd number by 5, the product is always odd.

When you multiply an even number by 5, the product is always even.

Page 30

1. 3 hundreds, 4 tens, 2 ones
2. 7 hundreds, 8 tens, 0 ones
3. 9 hundred, 1 tens, 2 ones
4. 8 hundreds, 0 tens, 5 ones
5. 9 hundreds, 2 tens, 6 ones
6. 4 hundreds, 5 tens, 9 ones
7. 6 hundreds, 0 tens, 3 ones
8. 1 hundred, 6 tens, 7 ones

Page 31

8, 16, 24, 32, 40, 48, 56, 64, 72, 80

Page 32

1. 6
2. 5
3. 8
4. 3
5. 4
6. 7
7. 6
8. 9
9. 11

Page 33

A slime

Page 34

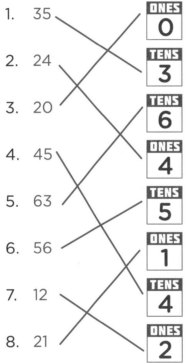

1. 35
2. 24
3. 20
4. 45
5. 63
6. 56
7. 12
8. 21

ONES 0
TENS 3
TENS 6
ONES 4
TENS 5
ONES 1
TENS 4
ONES 2

Page 35

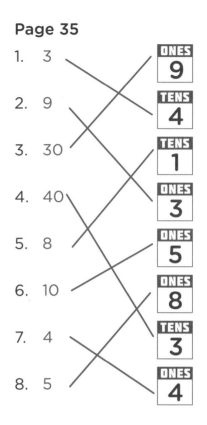

1. 3
2. 9
3. 30
4. 40
5. 8
6. 10
7. 4
8. 5

ONES 9
TENS 4
TENS 1
ONES 3
ONES 5
ONES 8
TENS 3
ONES 4

Page 36

A	B
1. 3×9=27	9. 9×7=63
2. 5×6=30	10. 4×6=24
3. 7×9=63	11. 3×11=33
4. 10×4=40	12. 6×5=30
5. 6×4=24	13. 9×3=27
6. 9×2=18	14. 4×10=40
7. 11×3=33	15. 2×6=12
8. 6×2=12	16. 2×9=18

The order in which you multiply two numbers does not affect the product.

Page 37

1. 12
2. 18
3. 10
4. 24
5. 20
6. 18
7. 27
8. 28

Page 38

1. 36; 40
2. 48; 50
3. 27; 30
4. 12; 10
5. 14; 10
6. 35; 40
7. 20; 20
8. 36; 40
9. 28; 30
10. 20; 20

Page 39

9, 18, 27, 36, 45, 54, 63, 72, 81, 90,

Page 40

1. 35 diamond swords
2. 24 pigs
3. 28 wood blocks
4. 18 TNT blocks

Page 41

1. 5 shelves
2. 10 apples
3. 9 arrows
4. 4 buckets of water

Page 42

1. 300 + 90 + 1
2. 700 + 50 + 6
3. 400 + 00 + 3
4. 100 + 80 + 6
5. 300 + 20 + 9
6. 100 + 60 + 0
7. 400 + 80 + 6
8. 300 + 20 + 9

Page 43

1. 3,000 + 200 + 10 + 4
2. 1,000 + 800 + 40 + 9
3. 6,000 + 700 + 00 + 4
4. 5,000 + 000 + 90 + 6
5. 9,000 + 100 + 30 + 2
6. 4,000 + 800 + 10 + 0
7. 3,000 + 000 + 20 + 1
8. 9,000 + 300 + 00 + 5

Page 44

1. 27
2. 45
3. 63
4. 72
5. 36
6. 9
7. 18
8. 54
9. 36
10. 27
11. 54
12. 9
13. 36
14. 81
15. 18

Page 45

1. 9
2. 6
3. 5
4. 4
5. 8
6. 10
7. 7
8. 3
9. 11

Give it a mirror

Page 46

1. 694
2. 37
3. 201
4. 830
5. 429
6. 504
7. 670
8. 934

Page 47

4, 8, 12, 16, 20, 24, 28, 32, 36, 40

Page 48

1. 63 ÷ 7 = 9
2. 24 ÷ 8 = 3
3. 36 ÷ 6 = 6
4. 20 ÷ 2 = 10
5. 54 ÷ 9 = 6
6. 35 ÷ 5 = 7
7. 24 ÷ 4 = 6
8. 27 ÷ 9 = 3
9. 25 ÷ 5 = 5

Page 49

1. $6 \times 3 = 18$
2. $7 \times 8 = 56$
3. $5 \times 6 = 30$
4. $10 \times 4 = 40$
5. $5 \times 9 = 45$
6. $4 \times 6 = 24$
7. $8 \times 8 = 64$
8. $10 \times 5 = 50$
9. $3 \times 9 = 27$

Page 50

1. 130; 1 hundreds, 3 tens, 0 ones
2. 540; 5 hundreds, 4 tens, 0 ones
3. 430; 4 hundreds, 3 tens, 0 ones
4. 920; 9 hundreds, 2 tens, 0 ones
5. 800; 8 hundreds, 0 tens, 0 ones
6. 340; 3 hundreds, 4 tens, 0 ones
7. 260; 2 hundreds, 6 tens, 0 ones
8. 310; 3 hundreds, 1 ten, 0 ones

It increases by one place value.

Page 51

1. 24; 20
2. 69; 70
3. 43; 40
4. 12; 10
5. 32; 30
6. 47; 50
7. 27; 30
8. 18; 20

Page 52

1. 4
2. 2
3. 1
4. Divide each slice in half
5. Divide each slice into thirds

Page 53

1. 9
2. 28
3. 5
4. 30
5. 7
6. 32
7. 6
8. 27
9. 8

Turn it upside down

Page 54

1. 3,841
2. 4,927
3. 6,041
4. 8,705
5. 342
6. 4,298

Page 55

11, 22, 33, 44, 55, 66, 77, 88, 99, 110

Page 56

2. $30 \div 10 = 3$
3. $63 \div 9 = 7$
4. $32 \div 4 = 8$
5. $28 \div 7 = 4$
6. $50 \div 10 = 5$
7. $36 \div 6 = 6$
8. $20 \div 10 = 2$
9. $81 \div 9 = 9$

Page 57

A coat of paint

Page 58

Wording will vary, but the equations should be as follows.

1. $5 \times 6 = 30$
2. $3 \times 6 = 18$
3. $6 \times 4 = 24$

Page 59

Wording will vary, but the equations should be as follows.

1. $28 \div 4 = 7$
2. $18 \div 6 = 3$
3. $12 \div 4 = 3$